American Law Enforcement in Trilingual:
English, Japanese, & Traditional Chinese

三か国語（英語・日本語・中国語繁体字）で見る

アメリカ法執行の仕事

美國執法部門——中日英三語對照（正體中文、日文、英文）

Miho Oda

Yu-Wen Lai

Wayne L. Davis, Ph.D.

BALBOA PRESS

A DIVISION OF HAY HOUSE

American Law Enforcement in Trilingual:
English, Japanese, & Traditional Chinese

三か国語（英語・日本語・中国語繁体字）で見
るアメリカ法執行の仕事

美國執法部門——中日英三語對照（正體中文、
日文、英文）

Authors, 著者, 作者

Wayne L. Davis, Ph.D. （ウェイン・L・デイヴィス博士,
韋恩•戴維斯 博士）

Miho Oda （小田実穂, 小田實穗）

Yu-Wen Lai （賴郁雯, 賴郁雯）

Illustrators, イラストレーター, 繪圖者

Brandon Lutterman, ブランドン・ラッターマン,

布蘭登 •路特曼

Ariana Greer, アリアナ・グリアー, 亞利安娜 •古雷爾

Derrick Freeman デリック・フリーマン, 德瑞克 •費曼

Christian Connolly, クリスチャン・コノリー,

科里遜・康諾利

Cover Photo: Yuan Peng, カバー写真：彭媛,

封面照片・彭

Balboa Press books may be ordered through booksellers or by contacting:

Balboa Press
A Division of Hay House
1663 Liberty Drive
Bloomington, IN 47403
www.balboapress.com
1 (877) 407-4847

Because of the dynamic nature of the Internet, any web addresses or links contained in this book may have changed since publication and may no longer be valid. The views expressed in this work are solely those of the author and do not necessarily reflect the views of the publisher, and the publisher hereby disclaims any responsibility for them.

The author of this book does not dispense medical advice or prescribe the use of any technique as a form of treatment for physical, emotional, or medical problems without the advice of a physician, either directly or indirectly. The intent of the author is only to offer information of a general nature to help you in your quest for emotional and spiritual well-being. In the event you use any of the information in this book for yourself, which is your constitutional right, the author and the publisher assume no responsibility for your actions.

Any people depicted in stock imagery provided by Thinkstock are models, and such images are being used for illustrative purposes only.
Certain stock imagery © Thinkstock.

ISBN: 978-1-5043-6910-7 (sc)
ISBN: 978-1-5043-7161-2 (hc)
ISBN: 978-1-5043-6911-4 (e)

Library of Congress Control Number: 2016919250

Print information available on the last page.

Balboa Press rev. date: 11/15/2016

Table of Contents, 目次, 目録

Preface

This book is designed for young readers. This book may be helpful to students who are learning multiple languages. This book presents information about U.S. local law enforcement work in three different languages (English, Japanese, and Traditional Chinese), which allow the students to make quick comparisons between the languages.

はじめに

この本は、若い読者向けに書かれたものです。多言語習得に取り組む学習者に役に立つように作られています。アメリカの法律の取り締まりをする仕事の内容や事情を三か国語（英語・日本語・中国語繁体字）で表して、学習者がさっと言葉の違いを比べられるようにしています。

序

這本書專門設計給青少年朋友閱讀。本書對於學習多國語言的學生將有所助益。本書以三種不同語言（英文、日文、正體中文）陳述美國警務工作的資訊，可使學生從中快速對照。

Declaration of Independence

According to the Declaration of Independence, the U.S. government derives its power from the people that it governs. Because there are more than 400 residents for every full-time police officer, social peace requires that people voluntarily comply with the law and assist with law enforcement efforts. Residents are stakeholders in maintaining a peaceful society and they must take an active part in promoting pro-social behaviors.

独立宣言

アメリカ独立宣言によると、合衆国政府は、国を治める一人ひとりによってその力を得ています。一人の警察官につき400人以上の居住者がいるため、社会の平和と安全のためには、人々が法律に従い、取り締まりに協力する必要があります。地域住民は、平和な社会を維持する上でお互いに影響しあう利害関係者であり、人の力になる行いを積極的にしなければなりません。

美國獨立宣言

根據美國獨立宣言，美國政府的權力來自其統治的人民。因為一名全職警察負責照顧超過四百個居民，社會安寧仰賴全民自發地遵守法律、協助法律執行成果。居民是對於維持和平社會之中有利害關係的人，他們必須積極提倡利社會行為，增進團體利益。

In CONGRESS, July 4, 1776.

The unanimous Declaration of the thirteen united States of America.

U.S. and State Constitutions

The U.S. Constitution is the supreme law in America involving federal law. Until the U.S. Supreme Court makes a ruling, federal laws may be different in different federal jurisdictions. Each state also has its own state constitution. A state constitution is the supreme law within a state involving state law. Different states have different laws.

アメリカ合衆国憲法および州憲法

米国憲法は、連邦法を含む、アメリカの最高法規です。合衆国の最高裁判所が裁定をするまでは、それぞれの連邦政府の管轄区域によって、連邦法がそれぞれ異なることもあります。各州にはそれぞれ独自の州憲法もあります。州憲法とは、その州の州法を含む中での最高法規です。州によって法律が異なります。

美國憲法與州憲法

美國憲法，包含聯邦法律，是在美國最有決定性的法律。直到最高法院裁決以前，聯邦法律在不同的聯邦管轄區域中可能會有所不同。每個州也有自己的州憲法。州憲法，包含州法律，是在所屬州裡具有最高決定權的法律。不同的州有不同的法律。

U.S. Constitution

The U.S. Constitution requires that police follow the law. The U.S. Constitution protects people's privacy. However, the U.S. Constitution only provides civilians with minimum protection. The states may provide civilians with more protection against the government.

アメリカ合衆国憲法

米国憲法は、警察官が法に従うよう命じています。米国憲法は人々のプライバシーを守ります。しかし、憲法は一般市民に最低限の保護しか提供していません。そのため、州が市民により手厚い保護を提供することもあります。

美國憲法

美國憲法要求警察守法。美國憲法保障人民的隱私。然而，美國憲法只提供市民最基本的保護。各州會提供更多保護市民不受政府欺負的法律。

Academy and Continual Training

Police cadets must attend and pass a law enforcement academy before they can become police officers. Police cadets study law, they train to help and protect people, and they learn to drive a police car under stressful conditions. Even after graduating from the police academy, police officers must continually train.

警察学校と継続的訓練

警察学校生徒は警察官になる前に法執行専門学校に通い、卒業しなければなりません。警察学校訓練生は法を学び、人々を守り、助けるために訓練をして、緊迫した状況下でもパトロールカーを運転できるようにします。専門学校を卒業したあとも、警察官は訓練をし続けなければいけません。

警察學校及後續培訓

警校學員必須進入執法學院受訓，畢業以後，才能成為警察。警校學生學習法律，他們受訓的目標是為了幫助、保護人們，他們還要學會在充滿壓力的情況下駕駛警車。即使警察從警校畢業了，他們仍然要持續學習。

City Police Officer

Here is a city police officer.

He is wearing a police uniform and a peaked cap.

He is wearing a badge on his uniform.

See the whistle chain leading to his right shirt pocket.

市街警察官
しがいけいさつかん

この人は市街警察官です。

警察の制服を着てハンチング（ひさし付の帽子）を被っています。

制服にバッジをつけています。

ホイッスルのチェーンが右のシャツのポケットにつながっているのが見えます。

城市警察

他是一個城市警察。

他穿著警察制服，戴著有帽舌的帽子。

他的制服上別著徽章。

看看這個口哨鏈子掛在他的右側衣服上。

Sheriff

Although the authority of a sheriff varies from jurisdiction to jurisdiction, the sheriff is an elected county official who is the chief law enforcement officer in any given county. A sheriff department oversees the county jail, provides security for courtrooms and judges, and delivers civil papers, such as jury summons and subpoenas.

郡保安官

郡保安官の権限は管轄地区によって様々あります が、保安官は、その郡で法執行官長として選ばれた 官職です。保安官部署は、郡刑務所を監督し、法廷と 裁判官の安全を確保し、陪審員召喚状や召喚状な ど市民への書類を届けます。

縣治安官

儘管各個管轄區內的縣治安官的職責權力，差異很大，縣治安官是在所在郡內選舉獲選的官員，他是當地最主要的執法者。一個縣治安部門監督郡立監獄，保障審判室和法官的安全，傳遞民事訴狀，例如審判傳喚狀，以及傳票。

Corrections Officer

Here is a county corrections officer.

She works for the sheriff department.

The sheriff, an elected official, runs the county jail.

She works inside the jail and watches inmates.

矯正官
<ruby>矯正官<rt>きょうせいかん</rt></ruby>

この<ruby>女性<rt>じょせい</rt></ruby>は<ruby>郡<rt>ぐん</rt></ruby>の<ruby>矯正官<rt>きょうせいかん</rt></ruby>です。

<ruby>彼女<rt>かのじょ</rt></ruby>は<ruby>保安課<rt>ほあんか</rt></ruby>で<ruby>働<rt>はたら</rt></ruby>いています。

<ruby>保安官<rt>ほあんかん</rt></ruby>は<ruby>公式<rt>こうしき</rt></ruby>に<ruby>選出<rt>せんしゅつ</rt></ruby>され、<ruby>郡<rt>ぐん</rt></ruby>の<ruby>刑務所<rt>けいむしょ</rt></ruby>を<ruby>管理<rt>かんり</rt></ruby>します。

<ruby>彼女<rt>かのじょ</rt></ruby>は<ruby>刑務所内<rt>けいむしょない</rt></ruby>で<ruby>受刑者<rt>じゅけいしゃ</rt></ruby>の<ruby>監視<rt>かんし</rt></ruby>をしています。

縣校軍官

她是一個縣校軍官。

她替縣治安官部門工作。

縣治安官是由選舉選出的官員，她負責管理該縣的監獄。

她在監獄裡工作，看管監獄犯人。

Bailiff

A bailiff is a peace officer who provides court security.   The bailiff ensures the safety of trial participants, provides assistance to judges, handles court documents, and enforces courtroom rules of behavior. The bailiff also announces the judge's entrance into the courtroom and provides jury escort outside of the courtroom to prevent jury contact with the public.

廷吏

廷吏とは、裁判所の警備をする保安官です。廷吏は裁判の安全を保証し、裁判官の補助をし、裁判の文書を扱い処理します。法廷の入り口で裁判官の入場を知らせたり、陪審員が法廷の外で公衆との接触を防ぐために、陪審員の付き添いもします。

法警

法警保障法院的和平。法警確保參與審判者的安全、協助法官、處理法院文件、強制執行法庭行為規範。此外，法警的工作還包含宣佈法官進入法庭，以及在法庭外護送陪審團，避免陪審團與公眾接觸。

State Trooper

Here is a state trooper.

He is wearing a campaign hat.

He has a police radio microphone on his left shoulder.

州警察官
しゅうけいさつかん

この人は州警察官です。

キャンペーンハットと呼ばれる帽子を被っています。

左の肩に警察官用のワイヤレスマイクをつけています。

州警察

這是一個州警察。

他戴一頂寬邊氈帽。

在他的左肩上，佩戴一個警察專用電台的麥克風。

Conservation Officers

A conservation officer is sometimes called a game warden. A conservation officer is a police officer who protects wildlife and the environment.   They protect game, catch poachers, and protect streams from being polluted. They also make sure that people enjoy the wilderness in a safe manner.

保全担当官

保全担当官は、猟区管理者と呼ばれることもあります。保全担当官は野生動物や環境を守る警官です。猟の対象になる動物を守り、密猟者を捕まえ、川を汚染から守ります。自然が保たれている地域を人々が安全に楽しめるようにも注意しています。

環保官員

環保官員有時也稱作「野生動物保護區管理員」。環保官員是保護野生動物和環境的警察。他們保護動物、抓盜獵者,避免溪流被污染。他們也保障人民可以安全地享受大自然環境。

Patrol Officers

Some police officers ride around in police cars. The officers keep an eye out for crime and traffic violations. Officers listen to many different radios, including the high frequency police radio, the low frequency police radio, and the CB radio. The dispatcher at the post will use a police radio, computer, or phone to inform the officer of a work detail and where to go. A work detail may include diffusing a volatile situation, interviewing a witness, protecting a hazardous scene, or recovering found items.

パトロール隊

パトロールカーで巡回する警察官がいます。警察官は

犯罪や交通違反に目を光らせています。警察官は警察用の

高周波無線、低周波無線、市民ラジオを含めたたくさんの無線

を聴きます。署にいる情報の発信者は警察無線コンピュータ

ー、または電話で警官に仕事の詳細や行先を伝えます。業務

の詳細には、一触即発の状況を鎮めたり、目撃者への聞

き込み、危険な現場での保護、見つかった物を返すことなども

含まれます。

Patrol Officers

Some police officers ride around in police cars. The officers keep an eye out for crime and traffic violations. Officers listen to many different radios, including the high frequency police radio, the low frequency police radio, and the CB radio. The dispatcher at the post will use a police radio, computer, or phone to inform the officer of a work detail and where to go. A work detail may include diffusing a volatile situation, interviewing a witness, protecting a hazardous scene, or recovering found items.

巡邏警察

有些警察坐在警車裡四處巡視。這些巡邏警察搜尋犯罪和交通違規。警員會聽許多不同的廣播電台，包含高頻率警察電台、低頻率警察電台，與民用波段電台（Citizen Band Radio）。負責發送公告的派遣員會使用警用電台、電腦、電話，通知警員工作上的細節以及要到哪裡去。工作上的細節包含通知違規情況、面談目擊證人、保護危險的犯罪現場，或復原找到的物件。

Traffic Direction Cops

Some police officers stand on busy street corners and direct traffic. The officers may use whistles, flashlights, and reflective traffic sticks to control the movement of cars. After the traffic in a particular direction has been stopped, the officers will allow people to safely walk across the street. These police officers work in rain, sleet, snow, and extreme heat.

交通取締官

交通量の多い道路の隅に立って通行を指揮する

警察官もいます。ホイッスルや、懐中電灯、交通整理用

の反射スティックを使って車の往来を調整します。取締

官は、ある方向の車の往来が止められたあとに、歩行者が

安全に道を渡れるようにします。彼らは雨や雪や厳しい暑

さのなかで働いています。

交通指揮警察

有些警察站在忙碌的街頭角落，指揮交通。交通警察會使用哨子、手電筒、反光指揮棒來控制車流。在某一個方向的車子都停下來以後，警察會讓行人安全地過馬路。這些交通警察在雨中、雪中、雨雪交加，或是極炎熱的天氣下工作。

Motorcycle Cops

Some police officers ride motorcycles. Motorcycles are more maneuverable than police cars, which may be advantageous on crowded streets. A motorcycle's relatively small size allows it to get to a crash scene more quickly than a police car when traffic is congested. Because motorcycles are smaller and lighter than cars, they are more fuel and cost efficient. Officers who ride motorcycles focus on traffic violations. They stop cars for going too fast, following too close, and disregarding traffic signals. The officers may write these drivers tickets.

オートバイ警察官

オートバイに乗る警察官もいます。オートバイはパトロールカーより狭い場所でも移動しやすく、混雑した道路で便利なことがあります。オートバイが比較的小さいことで、交通が混雑しているときにもより早く衝突現場へたどりつくことができます。オートバイは車よりも小さく軽いため、燃料と費用を少なく抑えることができます。オートバイに乗る警察官は交通違反を集中的にみます。速度が速すぎる車、車間距離が短すぎる車や、信号無視をした車を止めます。彼らは運転手に違反切符を切ることができます。

Motorcycle Cops

Some police officers ride motorcycles. Motorcycles are more maneuverable than police cars, which may be advantageous on crowded streets. A motorcycle's relatively small size allows it to get to a crash scene more quickly than a police car when traffic is congested. Because motorcycles are smaller and lighter than cars, they are more fuel and cost efficient. Officers who ride motorcycles focus on traffic violations. They stop cars for going too fast, following too close, and disregarding traffic signals. The officers may write these drivers tickets.

摩托車警察

有些警察騎摩托車。摩托車比起警用汽車更好操控，而且在擁擠的道路上更佔優勢。與汽車相比，摩托車相對較小的體積，可以讓警察在塞車時更快到達車禍現場，而且節省汽油支出。摩托車警察專門處理交通違規。他們會擋下行進速度過快的、跟車跟得太近的、違反交通號誌的車輛。這些警員能開不守秩序的駕駛罰單。

FREEMAN

Mounted Police

In some areas, police officers ride horses. In some jurisdictions, horses are considered vehicles. Police officers who ride horses are called mounted police. Horses can carry police officers where cars and motorcycles cannot go, such as in parks and in rough terrain areas. This may be essential for search and rescue efforts. Horses give police officers added height and visibility. The weight of a horse allows police officers to disperse unruly crowds.

騎馬警察官

ある地域では、馬に乗る警察官もいます。管轄区によっ

ては、馬は乗り物とみなされることもあります。馬に乗る

警察官は、騎馬警察官と呼ばれます。馬は、警察官を乗せ

て、車でもオートバイでも行けない公園やでこぼこと起伏が激

しいところまでたどり着くことができます。それが捜索活動や

救助活動に必要不可欠になることもあります。馬に乗ること

で、警察官は高いところから景色を見渡すことができます。馬の

重量によって、警察官は手に負えないような人ごみを分散

させることができます。

Mounted Police

In some areas, police officers ride horses. In some jurisdictions, horses are considered vehicles. Police officers who ride horses are called mounted police. Horses can carry police officers where cars and motorcycles cannot go, such as in parks and in rough terrain areas. This may be essential for search and rescue efforts. Horses give police officers added height and visibility. The weight of a horse allows police officers to disperse unruly crowds.

騎警

在某些地區的警察需要騎馬。在有些管轄區域裡，馬匹算是車輛的一種。騎著馬的警察被稱作騎警。馬兒可以帶警察到一些汽車與摩托車不能到的地方，例如公園和崎嶇的地帶。這對於搜救尤其重要。馬兒可以增加警察的高度，讓警察有更好的視野。馬兒的重量可讓警察驅散難以控制的群眾。

Police Aviation – Helicopters

Some police officers fly in helicopters. A helicopter has wings that rotate. Helicopters can hover and they can land in tight spaces. Police officers in helicopters watch for traffic jams and crashes on busy roadways. Helicopters have infrared, which allows the officers to see objects in the dark.

航空警察官　ヘリコプター

ヘリコプターに乗る警察官もいます。ヘリコプターには回転する翼がついています。空中の一定のところに浮き留まることができ、狭い場所でも着陸できます。ヘリコプターに乗る警察官は交通渋滞や交通量の多い道路の衝突を注意して見ます。ヘリコプターには赤外線がついているので、警察官は暗い中も見ることができます。

航空警察——直升機

有些警察駕駛直升機。直升機有旋轉的機翼。直升機可以在空中盤旋，而且能降落在較小的空間。航空警察坐在直升機裡，觀察擁塞交通和繁忙道路的車禍。直升機配有紅外線，能讓警察在黑暗中看得清楚。

Police Aviation - Airplanes

Some police officers fly in airplanes. An airplane has fixed wings that do not rotate. Compared to helicopters, airplanes can travel faster, farther, higher, and can be operated at a much lower cost. An airplane can be used to clock a vehicle's speed on the roadway by seeing how long it takes for the car to travel between two fixed points (speed = distance / time).

航空警察官　航空機

飛行機に乗る警察官もいます。飛行機には固定されて回転しない翼がついています。ヘリコプターと比べて、飛行機はより早く、遠く、高く移動し、より安い費用で操作することができます。航空機は、車両のスピードを、道路上のある二点間の移動速度を見ることで測ることができます。（速さ＝道のり÷時間）

航空警察——飛機

有些警察駕駛飛機。飛機有固定的機翼，機翼不會旋轉。與直升機相比，飛機飛得更快、更遠、更高，而且操作的花費比較低。藉著觀察汽車通過兩個定點之間需花費多長時間，一架飛機可以測量路面車輛的速度。

Bicycle Patrol

Some police officers ride on bicycles. Bike officers can travel faster and farther than foot patrol officers, they are able to patrol areas unreachable by car, they have a stealth advantage because they are silent, and they are cost effective. Bike patrol is very effective during special events, such as parades. Bicycles allow officers to better interact with the public, which is important for developing relationships. Police-community relationships are essential because community members have important knowledge that is essential for finding solutions to local problems.

自転車パトロール

自転車にのる警察官もいます。自転車警察官は歩いてパトロールする警察官よりも早く遠くまで移動することができ、車ではたどり着けない場所まで行き、静かなのでこっそりと、費用面でも効率的に巡回することができます。自転車でのパトロールは、パレードなどの特別な行事の時にとても効果的です。自転車に乗ることで、警察官は公衆との関係を築くために大切な、ふれあいの機会を持つことができます。地元の住民には、その地域での問題解決に役に立つ知識があることが多いので、警察官と地域の人々との関係は重要です。

Bicycle Patrol

Some police officers ride on bicycles. Bike officers can travel faster and farther than foot patrol officers, they are able to patrol areas unreachable by car, they have a stealth advantage because they are silent, and they are cost effective. Bike patrol is very effective during special events, such as parades. Bicycles allow officers to better interact with the public, which is important for developing relationships. Police-community relationships are essential because community members have important knowledge that is essential for finding solutions to local problems.

自行車巡邏警察

有些警察騎自行車。比起徒步巡邏的警察，自行車巡警移動速度較快，也可以到達較遠的地方，他們能在一些汽車到不了的地方巡邏。由於騎自行車很安靜，所以佔有隱秘的優勢，在開銷方面也比較省錢。在特別的場合下，例如遊行，騎自行車巡邏很有效率。自行車巡邏可讓警察更容易與公眾互動，是警察發展社區關係的重要環節。

Maritime Police

Maritime police officers patrol in watercraft. Their patrol areas may be coastal canals, rivers, lakes, harbors, and/or sea waters. They can reach locations not easily accessible by land. Maritime police officers promote the safety of water users by enforcing laws related to water traffic. Maritime police guard things on the dock, protect maritime animals, and prevent smuggling.

海洋警察官

海洋警察官は舟艇で水上を巡回する警察官です。巡回地域は海岸の入江、河川、湖、港、または海です。陸からは簡単に近づけない場所までたどり着くことができます。海洋警察官は水上交通に関する法律を守らせることで水上利用者の安全を奨励しています。埠頭のものを見張り、海洋動物を守り、密輸を防止します。

海警

海警開船巡邏。他們巡邏的區域包含沿海運河、河流、湖、港口、（或）海。他們能去一些從陸地不容易到達的地方。海警執行涉及海上交通的法律，藉此促進海上使用者的安全。海警保衛碼頭上的物品，保護海洋動物，並預防走私。

Canine Officer

Canine (K-9) officers go to a special school and learn how to work with dogs. Canines (dogs) have a much better sense of smell than do humans. Officers use their dogs to search for drugs, accelerants, explosives, cadavers, evidence, and missing people. Police officers and their dogs become very close and they work together as a team. The police dog is considered a police officer.

警察犬指導士

警察犬(Canine の発音は K-9：ケイナイン)指導士は特別な養成所に通い、犬との活動の仕方を習得します。イヌ科の動物(犬)は人間よりもずっと優れた嗅覚を持っています。警察官は薬物、燃焼促進剤、爆発物、死体、証拠物や行方不明者の捜索のため警察犬を扱います。警察官と警察犬はとても親密になり、チームとして共に働きます。警察犬は警察官としてみなされます。

Canine Officer

Canine (K-9) officers go to a special school and learn how to work with dogs. Canines (dogs) have a much better sense of smell than do humans. Officers use their dogs to search for drugs, accelerants, explosives, cadavers, evidence, and missing people. Police officers and their dogs become very close and they work together as a team. The police dog is considered a police officer.

警犬警員

警犬（英文 canine 的諧音：K-9）警員去專門學校學習如何與狗一起工作。狗的嗅覺比起人類靈敏許多。警員會利用狗來搜尋毒品、燃燒促進劑、炸藥、屍體、證物，和失蹤人口。警員與他們的警犬關係緊密，而且他們在同個團隊工作。警犬被視為警察的一員。

Evidence Officer

The evidence officer is responsible for the intake, storage, and disposal of all property collected by the department. The officer ensures that evidence is secure from theft, loss, and contamination. The officer transports property to the crime lab, maintains chain of custody reports, notifies property owners when they can get their property back, and coordinates the court-ordered disposal of contraband.

証拠品の管理担当員

その警察署が集めた、すべての署の所有物の受け入れ、保管、処分を担当します。警察官は証拠品が盗まれたり、失くしたり、汚れる危険がないように気をつけます。所有物を科学犯罪研究所へ運んだり、一連の管理報告書を保存したり、その物の持ち主にいつ返却されるか知らせたり、裁判所の密輸品処分命令を調整する作業をします。

證據官

證據官負責納入、儲存、丟棄所有部門搜集來的證物。證據官確保證物免於偷竊、遺失和污染。證據官運送證物到犯罪實驗室，維持保管記錄的正確性，通知證物持有者何時可以拿回他們的物品，以及協調法院明令需丟棄的走私物。

Scuba Divers

Some police officer are scuba divers. They are specially trained in underwater rescue, underwater recovery, and underwater investigation. Scuba divers carry their own source of air on their back, which allows them to breathe underwater. Police divers might need to dive in murky, dark, cold water with strong currents and parasites. Scuba divers must be able to swim.

スキューバダイバー

スキューバダイビングをする警察官もいます。彼らは水中での救助、復旧作業、調査のための特別な訓練を積んでいます。水中でも呼吸ができるように背中に酸素を積んでいます。ダイビングをする警察官は濁って暗く、冷たく強い海流や寄生生物のいる中でも潜水する必要があります。スキューバダイバーは泳げなければなりません。

浮潛警員

有些警察是浮潛員。他們接受海底救援、修復、調查的特訓。浮潛警員背著氧氣筒，這可使他們在海裡呼吸。浮潛警員有可能必須潛入污濁、黑暗、冰冷，且帶有潮流和寄生蟲的水裡。浮潛警員必須會游泳。

Snowmobile Officers

Snowmobiles allow police officers to respond to emergencies in snow storms. During blizzards, cars may get stuck on the roadway. The snow becomes too deep and the roadway becomes very slippery. Snowmobiles allow police officers to travel along impassable roadways in order to aid stranded motorists. Snowmobiles also allow police officers to travel off road and onto ice-covered lakes.

スノーモービル隊

スノーモービルがあれば、警察官は緊急時に吹雪の中でも動くことができます。暴風雪の中では道路で車が立ち往生してしまうことがあります。雪が積もりすぎると道路はとても滑りやすくなります。警察官は、取り残された運転手を救助するために、通れなくなった道をスノーモービルで移動します。スノーモービルは道を外れて氷が張った湖の上を走ることもできます。

雪地車警員

雪地車可讓警察在暴風雪時，針對急難狀況做出回應。暴風雪時，車子可能會困在路上。雪積得更深，而道路變得更滑。雪地車能讓警察穿越無法通行的道路，救援受困的駕駛人。雪地車也能帶警察到沒有柏油路的地方，甚至是冰雪覆蓋的湖面上。

School Resource Officers

Some police departments assign police officers to work within public schools. These police officers are called school resource officers. School resource officers are responsible for providing security and crime prevention services within the educational environment. The school resource officer has three main responsibilities: teacher, counselor, and law enforcement officer.

学校警備援助官
<small>がっこうけいびえんじょかん</small>

公立学校で 働 くように任命された警察官もいます。このような警察官は学校警備援助官と呼ばれます。

教 育現場で安全の 供 給 と犯罪の防止業務を提 供 する責務があります。彼らは教師であり、カウンセラーであり、法執行官であるという三つの役割を担っています。

School Resource Officers

Some police departments assign police officers to work within public schools. These police officers are called school resource officers. School resource officers are responsible for providing security and crime prevention services within the educational environment. The school resource officer has three main responsibilities: teacher, counselor, and law enforcement officer.

駐校警察

有些警察局會指派警察到公立學校。這些警察稱為駐校警察。駐校警察負責校園安全以及預防犯罪駐校警察身兼三項責任：老師、咨詢員、及執法人員。

Public Information Officers

The police department's professional reputation and the public's support depend on good police-media relations. The police are accountable to the public and the media are the community watchdogs. When a crisis event occurs, the police must have a trained public relations officer readily available to communicate with the media. The police need to monitor the messages that the media deliver to the public.

広報担当警察官

警察署のプロとしての評判と国民からの支持を得るには、警察とメディアとの間で良好な関係を築けるかどうかにかかっています。警察官は国民に説明責任を負っており、メディアは地域社会の番犬です。何か重大な事態に直面したとき、警察官はメディアとやりとりするために訓練され、すぐに対応できる広報担当官がいなければなりません。そしてメディアが公表する内容をチェックしなければなりません。

公關警察

警察局的聲譽和民眾支持度，有賴於警察與媒體之間的良好關係。警察對公眾負責，而媒體是社區的監察人。緊急事件發生時，一定會有專門負責公共關係的警察與媒體溝通。警察必須監控媒體傳達給大眾的訊息。

SWAT Officers

Some police departments may have a special weapons and tactics (SWAT) team. SWAT officers are specially trained to intervene in high-risk and dangerous situations. When patrol officers are overwhelmed and need emergency help, the SWAT team may be called to assist.

SWAT隊員

警察署によってはSWATチーム（特殊火器戦術部隊、Special Weapons And Tactics）があることもあります。SWAT隊員はとても危険性の高い状況に介入するために訓練されます。パトロール隊が大変な事態で緊急の助けが必要なとき、SWATチームが支援に呼ばれます。

特種武器和戰術部隊

某些警察局會有特種武器和戰術部隊，簡稱SWAT特種警察部隊。特種警察部隊受過特訓，專門處理高風險、危險的任務。當巡邏警察忙不過來，需要緊急協助時，特種警察部隊會被請來幫忙。

Bomb Squad Officer

A bomb squad officer is trained to find, approach, handle, and neutralize packages that may contain powerful explosives. A bomb squad officer will don a special bomb suit that will protect the officer from a blast. Tools used by bomb squad officers may include robots, mirrors, canines, x-ray devices, disrupter guns, laser scopes, bomb baskets, bomb cylinders, and special bomb trucks.

爆弾処理警察官

爆弾処理班の警察官は強力な爆発物が入っている可能性がある物を見つけ、近づいて、処理し、爆発物を無力化する訓練を受けています。爆弾処理班は特別な防爆スーツを身に着けます。使われる道具としては、ロボット、鏡、警察犬、X線機器、かく乱銃、レーザースコープ、爆弾バスケット、爆弾シリンダーや特殊爆弾トラックがあります。

拆彈警察小組官員

拆彈警組官員受過專門訓練，他們尋找、接近、處理、摧毀可能含有強大炸藥的包裹。拆彈警組官員會穿特殊的防彈衣，以保護他們免於炸彈衝擊。他們使用的工具包含機器人、鏡子、警犬、X射線裝置、拆彈用水波槍、雷射檢測鏡、防爆罐、彈筒，與專門放炸彈的卡車。

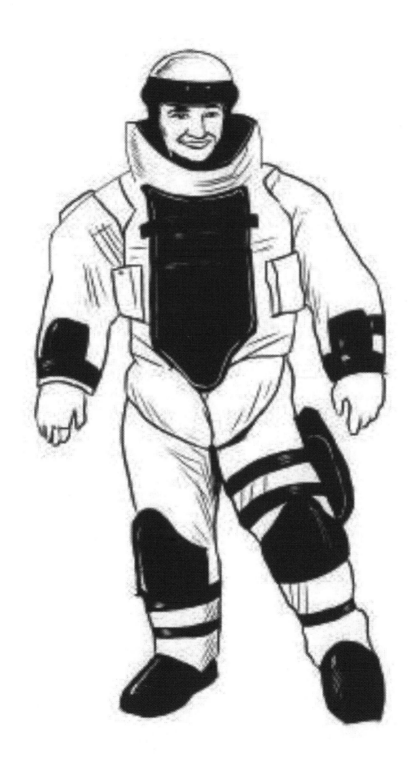

Defensive Tactics Instructor

In the U.S., there are rules for the type and amount of force that police officers can legally use against offenders to overcome resistance. A defensive tactics instructor is a certified officer who trains police officers in the proper use of force. In addition to their hands and feet, tools used by defensive tactics instructors include striking pads, handcuffs, batons, pepper spray, and training guns.

守備戦術インストラクター

アメリカでは、攻撃者の抵抗に打ち勝つために警察官が合法的に使える力の種類や程度に関するルールがあります。守備戦術講師は、警察官に適切な武力を使えるよう訓練をするために認定を受けた警察官です。手足に加え、守備戦術講師が扱う道具には、打撃吸収パッド、手錠、警棒、唐辛子スプレーやトレーニング用銃があります。

防守戰術指導員

在美國，警察可合法用來對抗侵犯者的武力，針對這種防禦，有種類和數量的規範。防守戰術指導員是通過認證的警員，負責訓練警察使用適當的武力。除了使用他們的手腳以外，防守戰術指導員還會使用拳擊擋板、手銬、指揮棒、胡椒噴霧，以及訓練用槍。

Crash Investigators

Police officers investigate vehicle crashes. Police officers want to know why each crash happened. An officer will use a measuring wheel to measure distances and a protractor or compass to measure angles. It is not always possible to measure all the distances and angles due to the terrain. However, math can be used to calculate the missing variables. A drag sled can be used to measure road surface friction. With this information, the speed and direction of the vehicles can be calculated prior to the collision.

衝突事故の取り調べ人

警察官は乗り物の衝突事故を取り調べます。なぜ衝突が起きたのか知る必要があります。距離を測るための車輪付き測定器や、角度を測るための分度器やコンパスを使います。地形によっては、すべての距離や角度を測ることが必ずしもできるわけではありません。それでも、数学を使って欠けている部分を計算することができます。路面摩擦を測定するために、そりが使われることがあります。この資料を使って、衝突前のスピードや乗物の方向が計算されます。

Crash Investigators

Police officers investigate vehicle crashes. Police officers want to know why each crash happened. An officer will use a measuring wheel to measure distances and a protractor or compass to measure angles. It is not always possible to measure all the distances and angles due to the terrain. However, math can be used to calculate the missing variables. A drag sled can be used to measure road surface friction. With this information, the speed and direction of the vehicles can be calculated prior to the collision.

車禍調查警員

警察調查車禍。他們希望知道每場車禍發生的原因。警察會使用測量輪和量角器或指南針來測量角度。依據不同地帶，並不是每次都能測量所有的距離和角度。但是，數學可用來計算遺失的變量。拖動雪橇可用來測量路面的摩擦。有了這項資訊，車輛的速度及方向就可在擦撞前被計算出來。

Crash Reconstructionist

A crash reconstructionist is a police officer who has received specialized training to investigate serious vehicle crashes. The officer will use scientific processes to identify the causes of a crash by considering the vehicle design, vehicle damage, speed of operation, lamp filaments, yaw marks, the roadway, and the environment. Officers use mathematics and physics to determine fault and to assign blame.

衝突現場復元員

衝突現場復元員は、大きな車の衝突の取り調べをするための特別な訓練を受けた警察官です。車のデザインや損傷、運転速度、（ヘッド）ライト、タイヤ跡、車道や周囲の状況をよく精査して原因を突きとめるために科学的な方法を用います。数学や物理を使って過失を判断し責任を問います。

Crash Reconstructionist

A crash reconstructionist is a police officer who has received specialized training to investigate serious vehicle crashes. The officer will use scientific processes to identify the causes of a crash by considering the vehicle design, vehicle damage, speed of operation, lamp filaments, yaw marks, the roadway, and the environment. Officers use mathematics and physics to determine fault and to assign blame.

事故現場重建警員

事故現場重建警員是受過特訓，專門調查嚴重車禍的警察。事故現場重建警員使用科學方法，諸如考量汽車的造型設計、汽車的損傷、駕駛車速、燈絲、偏航輪胎軌跡、道路及整體環境狀況等，以鑑識車禍發生的原因。事故現場重建警員也利用數學和物理來釐清責任歸屬，判定誰對誰錯。

Report Writing

Police officers write many different types of reports. Some of the reports include affidavits, crash reports, public service reports, intelligence reports, and case reports. Criminal reports are based on the elements of the law. English and math are required to properly interpret the law. Improper grammar will impact the truth value or meaning of the law. Police officers must use English and math to effectively write reports.

報告書作り

警察官はたくさんの種類の報告書を書きます。宣誓供述書、衝突報告書、社会奉仕活動報告書、情報報告者報告書、状況報告書などが含まれます。犯罪報告書は法律に基づいています。法律を正しく解釈するために英語と数学が必要不可欠です。文法が正しくないと、事実の信ぴょう性や法律の解釈に悪影響を与えてしまいます。警察官は英語と数学を効果的に使って報告書を書かなければなりません。

撰寫報告

警察撰寫各式各樣的報告。這些報告包含口供、車禍記錄、公共服務記錄、情報、案例報告。犯罪報告是基於「犯罪的要素」（證明被告者有罪的事實）。他們需要使用正確的英文和數學詮釋法律。不恰當的文法會影響事實的正確性或法律的意思。警察必須善用英文和數學來有效率地撰寫報告。

Latent Fingerprints

All fingerprints are unique. Once a fingerprint is collected, it can be used to identify the person who left it behind. Latent fingerprints are fingerprints left at a crime scene that may not be immediately visible to the naked eye. Police officers use magnetic and nonmagnetic colored powders to find the invisible fingerprints. Other techniques to find invisible fingerprints include superglue fumes and chemical sprays.

隠れた指紋

指紋には同じものがなく、みんな違っています。一度指紋が採取されると、それは誰が残したものなのかを明らかにするために使われます。犯罪現場の隠れた指紋とは、肉眼ではすぐに見えないような犯罪現場に残された指紋のことです。警察官は磁気を帯びたものと、そうでない色のついた粉を使って見えない指紋を探します。指紋を採取する他の手段としては、瞬間接着剤の煙や化学スプレーがあります。

潜在指紋

所有的指紋都是獨一無二的。一旦指紋被採集，它就可以用來識別是哪個人留下的。潜在指紋是在犯罪現場裡無法立即被肉眼察覺出來的指紋。警察使用磁性和非磁性彩色粉末來找到肉眼看不見的指紋。我們還可以利用強力膠煙霧和化學噴霧，找到看不見的指紋。

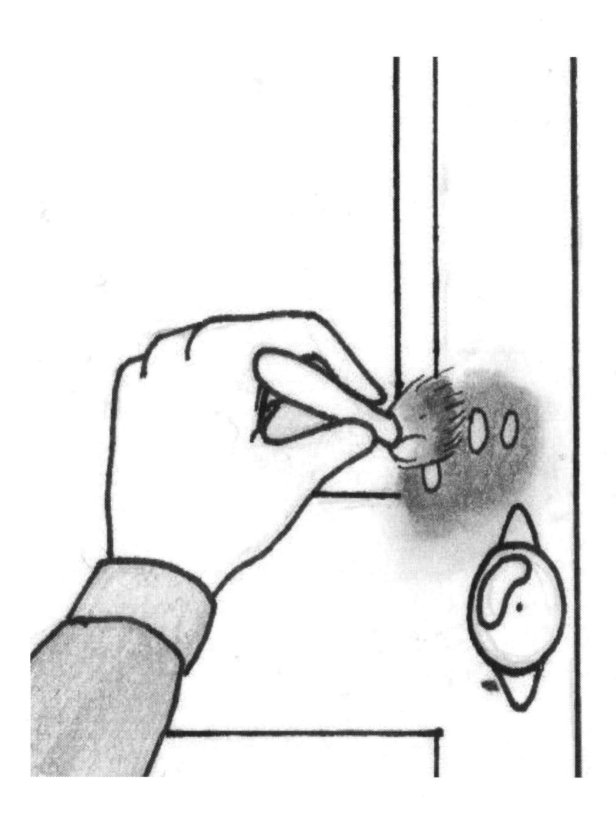

Rolling Fingerprints

Once an adult has been arrested by the police, a corrections officer will need to book the defendant into the jail. In order to properly identify the accused, a law enforcer will take the suspect's fingerprints. The officer will place each of the suspect's fingers into black ink and will then roll each finger onto a red fingerprint card. Some departments can perform this task electronically without ink. A blue fingerprint card is used for background checks and are not used for criminal purposes.

指紋の採取

成人が警察官に捕まると、矯正官は犯罪実行者を刑務所に入れる必要があります。きちんと犯罪実行者をつきとめるために、法執行官（警察官）は容疑者の指紋を採取します。警察官は容疑者それぞれの指紋を黒いインクにつけて赤い指紋カードに指をまわすようにつけます。署によっては、この作業はインクを使わず電子機器で済ますことができます。青い指紋カードは経歴確認のために使われ、刑事上の目的では使われません。

按壓指紋

一旦一名成年人被警察逮捕，縣校軍官將會送這個罪犯入獄。為了妥善辨別這個罪犯的身份，執法人員會採集這名嫌疑犯的指紋。警察會將嫌犯的指紋放入黑色墨水，然後按壓每個指頭到一張紅色的指紋卡上。有些部門利用電子設備按壓指紋，而不需要墨水。藍色的指紋卡用於身家背景調查，而不適用於犯罪者。

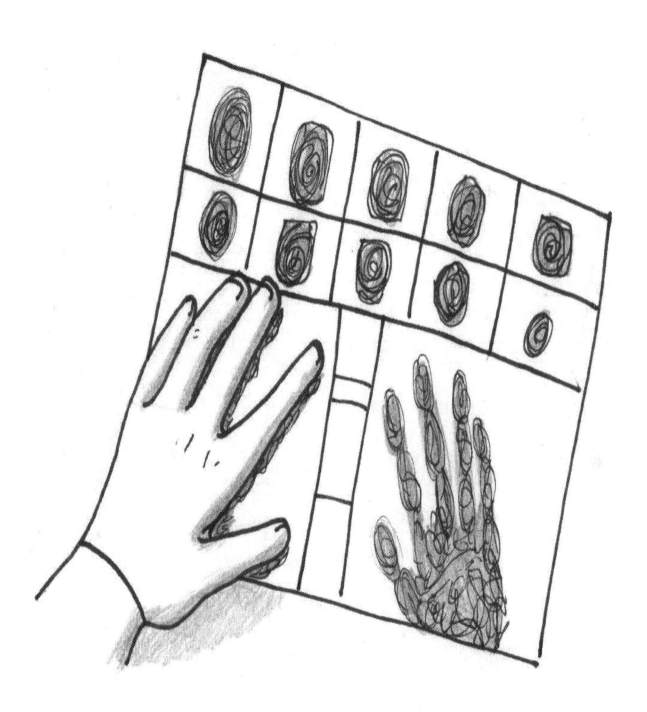

Interrogation

The police only need to be 51% confident that a crime occurred in order to make an arrest. Interrogation exists when a person is under arrest and is being questioned by police about the commission of a specific crime. When being interrogated, the person has a right to a lawyer and may stop answering questions at any time.

取り調べ

警察官は犯罪が起きたことを51%確信するだけで逮捕することができます。誰かが逮捕され、特定の犯罪を犯したことについて警察に質問をされるときに取り調べが行なわれます。尋問されたとき、人は弁護士を雇う権利を持っており、いつでも質問に答えるのをやめることができます。

審問

警察只要有51%的信心認定犯罪事件發生，就可以成立逮捕行動。審問就是當嫌疑犯遭到逮捕，被警察問訊是不是犯下特定罪行。嫌疑犯被審問時，他有權利申請律師陪同，並且能夠隨時拒絕回答問題。

DNA (deoxyribonucleic acid) Analysis

Police officers may need to collect DNA evidence at a crime scene. DNA is a person's genetic blueprint that can be used for identification purposes.   A person's bodily fluids, such as blood, contain DNA evidence. Blood can be collected via cotton swabs and placed into a cardboard box. Blood should not be placed into a plastic bag because it will putrefy and become ruined. Properly collected blood evidence can then be sent to the crime lab for DNA analysis. To maintain the integrity of the evidence, the police will seal the box and will use a chain of custody form to indicate all persons who have handled the evidence.

DNA鑑定

警察官は刑事事件ではDNAの証拠を集めなければならないことがあります。DNAとは、身元確認のために使われる人の遺伝子情報です。その人の身体の体液、例えば血液には証拠となるDNAが含まれています。血液は綿棒を使って採取され段ボール箱の中に入れられます。すぐに腐ってだめになってしまうので、血液はビニール袋には入れてはいけません。適切に採取された血液の証拠はDNA鑑定のために科学犯罪研究所へ運ばれます。証拠を完全な状態に保つために、警察官は箱にしっかり封をして、その証拠を扱ったすべての人を過程管理書に記します。

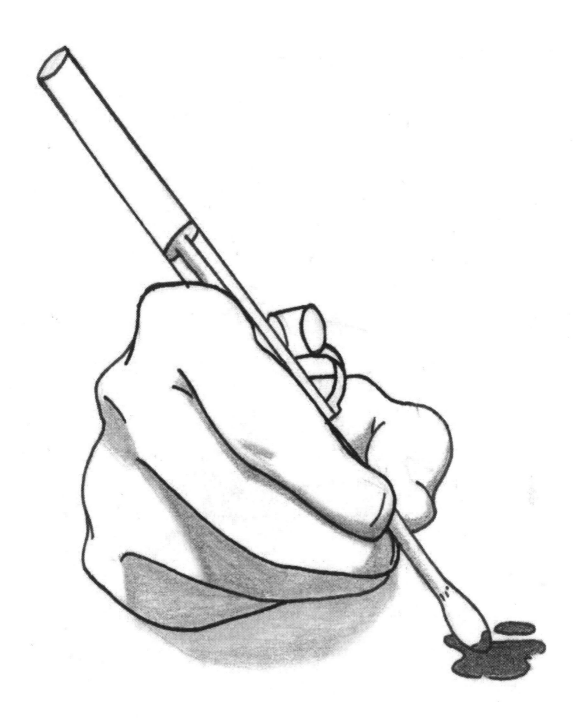

DNA (deoxyribonucleic acid) Analysis

Police officers may need to collect DNA evidence at a crime scene. DNA is a person's genetic blueprint that can be used for identification purposes. A person's bodily fluids, such as blood, contain DNA evidence. Blood can be collected via cotton swabs and placed into a cardboard box. Blood should not be placed into a plastic bag because it will putrefy and become ruined. Properly collected blood evidence can then be sent to the crime lab for DNA analysis. To maintain the integrity of the evidence, the police will seal the box and will use a chain of custody form to indicate all persons who have handled the evidence.

DNA（去氧核糖核酸）分析

警察有時需要在犯罪現場搜集 DNA 證據。DNA 是一個人的基因藍圖，可以用來鑑定身份。人類的體液，例如血液，含有 DNA。血液能透過棉花棒採集，放到硬紙箱裡。血液不該放進塑膠袋，因為它會在很短的時間內腐壞。利用適當方式搜集的血液會被送去犯罪實驗室進行 DNA 分析。為了維持證物完整性，警察會密封箱子，並使用一連串的保管表格，記錄有哪些人員經手過這個箱子。

Search Crime Scenes

Police officers search areas for lost people and items. The police need to have a plan of action in order to cover the area most efficiently and effectively. Different search techniques should be used for different purposes and different locations. Sometimes the police need to find a person in an unknown direction. Other times the police need to find a small item in a known area.

犯罪現場の調査

警察官は地域内で行方不明になった人や遺失物を探します。一番能率的に、そして効果的に地域をカバーできるように計画を立てる必要があります。いろいろな目的や場所によって様々な捜索手段が取られます。どの方角かもわからない所から人を探さなければならないときもあります。その他は、わかっているエリア内で小さな物や項目を見つけ出す必要があります。

捜尋犯罪現場

警察搜尋不同區域的失蹤人口與物品。警察需要行動計劃，好讓搜尋涵蓋區域更有效率。在不同的目的與區域，應該使用不同的搜尋技巧。有時候警察需要從一個未知的方向找一個人，有時警察需要在一個已知的地區找尋一個小物品。

School Presentations

Knowledge is a valuable tool. Police officers attempt to educate students to promote safety and health. Police officers may show videos and pass out brochures. Police officers may also let students wear inebriation goggles so that they can experience the disorientation effects caused by alcohol and drugs. The intoxication goggles are safe, fun to use, and do not cause drunkenness.

学校での取り組み

知識というのは役立つツールです。警察官は、生徒たちに安全と健康を奨励するための教育を企画します。そしてビデオを見せたりパンフレットを配ったりします。酩酊ゴーグルをかけることで、お酒や薬物による方向感覚の喪失効果を体験することができます。酩酊ゴーグルは安全で、楽しく、酒酔いを引き起こしません。

學校簡報

知識是寶貴的工具。警察試圖教育學生以提倡安全與健康意識。警察會播放影片和發送宣傳手冊。警察有時也會讓學生試戴「醉酒眼鏡」，好讓他們體驗酒精和毒品帶來的迷失方向感。醉酒眼鏡使用上安全、有趣，且不會造成醉酒。

Public Services

Police officers promote traffic safety and perform public services. When a car on the road gets a flat tire, a police officer can change the tire for the driver. Because it is unsafe for an occupied car to be parked on the berm, changing the tire helps fix the car so that it can be moved out of harm's way.

公衆への奉仕活動

警察官は交通安全や公衆へのサービス実践を促進しています。 車のタイヤが道路でパンクしたとき、警察官は運転手のためにタイヤを取り替えてあげます。人が乗った車が路肩に駐車されると危ないので、タイヤを交換して車を直すことで路肩から移動させることができます。

公共服務

警察提倡交通安全，執行公共服務。當一輛行駛中的車爆胎了，警察會幫駕駛換輪胎。因為停靠在路肩的車是不安全的，警察幫忙換輪胎可以讓車子早點移開路肩。

Fire Control

Some police officers are public safety officers who are trained in fire suppression. Police officers will use fire extinguishers to control fires. Police officers must use the right kind of fire extinguisher for each specific type of fire. For example, a water type fire extinguisher is appropriate for wood fires but is extremely dangerous for cooking oil fires. A carbon dioxide fire extinguisher is effective for cooking oil fires, but it does not work well for wood fires. Smoke from fires can be extremely hot and poisonous.

消火活動

消火活動をする訓練を受けた保安公務員である警察官もいます。火事の火を抑えるために消火器を使います。いろいろな火事の種類によって、それに適した消火器を使わなければなりません。例えば、水の消火器は森林火災には適していますが、調理用油が原因の火事には大変危険です。炭酸ガスの消火器は調理油には効果的ですが、森林火災には効果がありません。火事から出る煙はとても熱く、有毒であることもあります。

Fire Control

Some police officers are public safety officers who are trained in fire suppression. Police officers will use fire extinguishers to control fires. Police officers must use the right kind of fire extinguisher for each specific type of fire. For example, a water type fire extinguisher is appropriate for wood fires but is extremely dangerous for cooking oil fires. A carbon dioxide fire extinguisher is effective for cooking oil fires, but it does not work well for wood fires. Smoke from fires can be extremely hot and poisonous.

消防

有些警察負責公共安全，他們的職責是滅火。警察用滅火器控制火勢。警察一定要使用正確的滅火器以應對不同形式的火災。舉例來說，噴水式的滅火器適用於木材引起的火勢，但對於食用油導致的火災則非常危險。二氧化碳滅火器對於食用油導致的火災很有用，但對於木材引起的火勢則沒有幫助。火災產生的煙非常熱，而且具有毒性。

First Aid & CPR

Sometimes people need immediate medical assistance when no doctors are readily available. Police officers are trained in first aid and cardiopulmonary resuscitation (CPR). The American Red Cross offers first aid training. The ABCs of first aid are Airway, Breathing, and Circulation. Police officer are trained to use Automated External Defibrillators, a portable device that checks the heart rhythm and sends an electric shock to the heart, when needed, in an attempt to restore a normal rhythm. First aid includes simple procedures such as dressing a wound, setting a bone with a splint, treating a burn with ointment, and stopping blood loss by applying pressure. The goal is to preserve life, to prevent further harm, and to promote recovery.

応急手当と心肺蘇生法

その場に医師がいないときにも、即時の医療処置が必要な人がいます。警察官は応急手当てと心肺蘇生法（CPR）の訓練をしています。アメリカの赤十字が応急処置の訓練を提供しています。応急処置を覚えるためのABCは、Airway（気道確保）、Breathing（人工呼吸）、Circulation（血液循環、心臓マッサージ）です。警察官は、AED（自動体外式除細動器）を使えるように訓練を受けます。AEDは、心拍を確認し、必要があれば正常な心拍に戻すために心臓に電気ショックを送る携帯型の装置です。応急処置は、外傷の手当てや、骨折したところにあて木をしたり、火傷に軟膏をぬったり、圧迫して止血をしたりといった単純な処置を含みます。命を守り、これ以上の傷や痛みを防ぎ、回復を促すことが目的です。

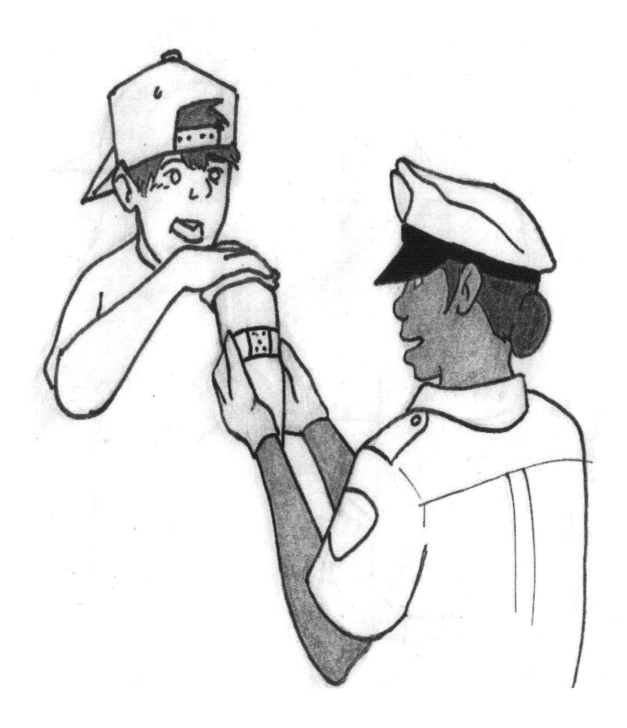

First Aid & CPR

Sometimes people need immediate medical assistance when no doctors are readily available. Police officers are trained in first aid and cardiopulmonary resuscitation (CPR). The American Red Cross offers first aid training. The ABCs of first aid are Airway, Breathing, and Circulation. Police officer are trained to use Automated External Defibrillators, a portable device that checks the heart rhythm and sends an electric shock to the heart, when needed, in an attempt to restore a normal rhythm. First aid includes simple procedures such as dressing a wound, setting a bone with a splint, treating a burn with ointment, and stopping blood loss by applying pressure. The goal is to preserve life, to prevent further harm, and to promote recovery.

急救與心肺復甦

在沒有醫生能馬上救援的情況，有時候人們需要即刻的醫療協助。警察受過由美國紅十字會提供的心肺復甦的訓練。最基礎的急救是 ABCs，A 就是 Airway （保持呼吸道暢通），B 就是 Breathing（人工呼吸），C 就是 Circulation（胸部按壓）。警察受過「自動體外心臟去顫器」的使用訓練。自動體外心臟去顫器是一種攜帶型裝置，可檢測心律，並在試圖維持心臟正常的律動時，發送電擊到心臟。急救包含了簡單的程序，例如包紮傷口、將骨頭用夾板固定、在燙傷處敷上藥膏、施壓止血以避免血液流失等。目的是保護生命、預防更嚴重的傷口，以及促進恢復速度。

Police Officers are Compatriots

Police officers are part of the local community. They are compatriots who have a vested interest in developing and maintaining a peaceful society. They have families and friends like everyone else. Police officers are peacemakers who have sworn to serve the public.

警察官も地域の一員

警察官は地域の一員です。彼らは発展し平和な社会を維持する既得権益をもっている同胞です。他の人と同じように、警察官にも家族や友人がいます。警察官は、公共のために奉仕すると誓った平和維持活動者なのです。

警察是同胞

警察是當地社區的一份子。在發展及維護和平社會上，他們是有既得利益的同胞。他們也像一般人一樣，擁有家庭和朋友。警察是宣誓過要服務大眾的和事佬。

Authors, <ruby>著者<rt>ちょしゃ</rt></ruby>, 關於作者

Wayne L. Davis, Ph.D.

Wayne L. Davis holds a Bachelor of Science in Electrical Engineering, a Master of Science in Business Administration, and a Ph.D. in Criminal Justice. Dr. Davis has graduated from city, state, and federal law enforcement academies and he has over 20 years of law enforcement experience with city, state, and federal law enforcement agencies. Dr. Davis was a field training officer with the Indiana State Police and has received the U.S. Customs & Border Protection Commissioner's Award.

ウェイン・L・デイヴィス博士

ウェイン・L・デイヴィスは電子工学の理学学士号、経営学の修士号、刑事司法の博士号を所持しています。デイヴィス博士は都市、州、および連邦法執行学校を卒業し、法執行機関で20年以上の経験があります。デイヴィス教授はインディアナ州警察の訓練官で、アメリカ税関・国境警備局長賞を受賞しました。

韋恩•戴維斯 博士

韋恩•戴維斯擁有電機工程學理學學士，企業管理理學碩士，和刑事司法博士學位。戴維斯博士畢業於城市級、州級，和聯邦級執法學院，而且他與上述機構共事超過二十年。戴維斯博士是訓練印第安那州州警察的專員，並且獲得美國海關邊防警長獎。

Miho Oda

Miho Oda holds a Bachelor of Arts in English Communication from Toyo University in Japan. She is a Teaching Associate of Japanese language at Lincoln Memorial University, where she is working on her Master's degree in Education.

おだみほ
小田実穂

とうようだいがくぶんがくぶえいご　がっか
東洋大学文学部英語コミュニケーション学科

そつぎょう　げんざい　だいがく
卒業。現在はリンカーンメモリアル大学にて

にほんご　こうし　つと　どうだいがくいん　きょういくがく
日本語の講師を務め、同大学院にて教育学を

せんこう
専攻しています。

小田實穗

小田實穗自日本東洋大學英語傳播學系取得學士學位，目前在林肯紀念大學擔任日語講師，並專攻教育學碩士。

Yu-Wen Lai

Yu-Wen Lai holds a Bachelor of Arts in Chinese Literature from National Chengchi University in Taiwan. She teaches Chinese Language and continues her master's degree at Lincoln Memorial University.

ライユウェン
賴郁雯

賴郁雯は台湾の国立政治大学にて中国文学の学士を取得しました。リンカーンメモリアル大学にて中国語を教え、修士課程に進んでいます。

賴郁雯

賴郁雯畢業於臺灣國立政治大學中國文學系，目前於美國林肯紀念大學擔任中文教師，以及攻讀碩士學位。

Printed in the United States
By Bookmasters